Confi... Your Arrow Fly

The Little Book of CrossFit for Beginners

IGNITE STRENGTH, DISCIPLINE
OF THE MIND, AND LIFE
LEADERSHIP

Heidi Leatherby, CF–L1

Confidence to Let Your Arrow Fly

The Little Book of CrossFit for Beginners

EVERYTHING HAS A BEGINNING

I would like to express heartfelt gratitude to you for holding in your hands, The Little Book of CrossFit for Beginners.

Not everyone is comfortable with the idea of walking into a new space with heavy weights booming as they crash to the floor, people performing unfamiliar physical monstrosities, and beads of sweat flying like little projectile missiles only to land in small splatters on whatever surface gets in their way. Enter the reasoning for why this little book was written. Here we have a short compilation of information for those curious about Crossfit. It is a carefully thought out and work in both physical and digital format for those interested enough to ask, but may not have an actual person to trust, on the subject. It is meant to give just enough of an overview to help one decide if this realm is right for the individual, and to provide a well-rounded understanding of this fitness community at a high level. I've also left plenty of room in various areas of the printed version of this book for your notes, as well as a few blank pages in the back for added thoughts, goals, and most importantly, accomplishments. Thank you once again for picking up this book, and I hope you enjoy it!

Heidi Leatherby

TABLE OF CONTENTS

INTRODUCTION

*"Every man's heart one day beats its final beat.
His lungs breathe their final breath. And if what
that man did in his life makes the blood pulse
through the body of others and makes them
believe deeper in something that's larger than
life, then his essence, his spirit, will be
immortalized by the storytellers - by the loyalty,
by the memory of those who honor him, and
make the running the man did live forever."*

- James Brian Hellwig

After researching for a long time, I could not find a
single book or collection of information to help
people get an idea of what it is like to be new in a
CrossFit gym, without having to actually step into
one. What we have here is simply a blueprint for
anyone to use if you are on the fence about giving
CrossFit a try, or if curious about it in any way. This
little book will not delve into the hundreds of stories,
studies, individual journeys of national competitors,
record holders, or detailed personal experiences of
mine, nor will it go into the depths of a specific diet
or food protocol. More on that in another book.

Instead, it is my hope that what is written here might give a quick, well rounded, and honest perspective from a person who began, like many people, from scratch. And, like many people who started, I continue to push through and improve without becoming a top competitor, CrossFit legend, or record holder. Dare I say that we actually do get hooked on the very thing that scares us away sometimes - the continuous opportunities for improvement, and the continuous ways in which we can observe ourselves and others become better and better with each obstacle we overcome.

Many people are intimidated by the idea of showing up at a gym full of strangers with a reputation for a coach barking and pushing athletes to the point of throwing up. Others may wonder why their neighbor or relative is going to this hole in the wall, dark, garage-like place with loud music and things that beep and clang and rattle. And furthermore, those indecipherable crashing sounds, the shaking noises that, if one dares to think about them, compare to what could be imagined if the inner crust of the earth were to open, shatter, and crash down (for all to pick back up, again of course. And then again, tomorrow). Day after day. Every morning, every afternoon, or whatever time they can make it to the gym, they do this. They drive, walk, bike, and even run to these places, take their marching orders from Captain White Board, only to emerge looking like quivering, sweaty heaps of bobbling limbs, again, for the fifth time that week. Every week.

I will say, it is not all that it seems. It might actually be better than what is illustrated above, and it's quite possible that sometimes it is far worse. But in all seriousness, I hope that the following might give some insight into what we do and how anyone can let a good coach help modify your experience to fit your own personal needs and goals.

And best of all, you will not have to sift through hundreds of pages of various books on the CrossFit subject to find one small gem buried within Able Amy's 500-page journey to the CrossFit Games or Cutthroat Carl's tips and tricks for a stellar thruster to back squat transition. And above all else, I hope to save you the dishonor of spending your last waking hours of the evening searching through gym rat forum pits of despair only to find very little on the subject of what it is actually like to step into your local CrossFit gym for the first time.

I can tell you what it is like to step into the local CrossFit gym for the first time, but I will refrain. The experience you have when entering that space for the first time, which will include a completely new set of sounds, smells, and energy, is all yours.

All I can say without feeling too guilty for sharing, is that it was, without a doubt, the thing that taught my arrow to fly. Fast, loud, heavy and hard.

CHAPTER 1

The Why

WE'RE ALL NEW IN THE BEGINNING

Greetings from a non-athlete. Not only a non-athlete, but someone who had zero competitive desire or inclination to participate in anything that had the slightest resemblance to the word 'sport 'or 'group. 'Or worst of all, 'partner. 'This, to my amusement still, was prior to joining a CrossFit gym at the age of 30. A couple of years later, something my past self would have thought was an outright joke, I earned my certificate as a Level 1 trainer.

Folks, here we have it. My best mile was a 16-minute atrocity in middle school, and all I could do was dangle like a helpless fish on a hook when asked to do one measly pull-up for the Presidential Fitness test. Into my late 20's, any rise in heart rate during a short-lived jog resulted in my lungs burning, and the taste of blood in my mouth. I came very close to tearing both Achilles tendons after the first session of a "beginners" running class, which put me out for almost an entire summer. Holding my hands above my head to attach a shower curtain to the rod made me see stars and feel as though I would pass out, and walking the company 5k was an absolute and resounding no unless I wanted shin splints to render me useless for a week afterward. Yoga seemed like a good idea, but was terribly deflating as my muscles never had enough juice to hold me up during the longer poses. I don't think I need many additional examples to drive the point home here: I wasn't in a very good starting place given the fact that everything remotely physically active resulted in the same thing. The conclusion was that I just wasn't going to get better. At any of it. Or so I let myself believe.

Then, I started noticing people in their 40's and 50's who had been inactive most of their lives, like me. Really noticing. And that's when it hit me. Crap, I was heading in this direction, and this is how it starts. It seemed to come out of nowhere too, with these people and their ailments. The onset of constant soreness and stiffness, the hobbling up and down stairs, groaning when getting in and out of vehicles, the doctor visits, and medication. A lot of medication, for the aches and pains or course. And then, the seemingly inevitable progression from soreness to knee and hip replacements, followed by the inability to bend down and lift a turkey out of the oven on Thanksgiving. Next came the loss of balance, falling and shattering bones. WALKING would then become a task for some. And on top of it all, the constant complaining about how bad they felt just seemed to take up more of any given conversation than anything else. This all seemed like a lot of work, to be honest. Much more work than getting myself into decent shape anyway. And let's face it, all of this certainly seemed more expensive than a gym membership.

Well, if I was afraid of not getting better at any of this physical activity stuff, I was absolutely terrified of becoming UNABLE to do it. When a friend of mine who was out of shape told me about their extremely positive experience with a local CrossFit gym, I decided to pick the lesser of two evils and give exercise a shot. Again.

What I found, I'm hoping might help others decide if training in this way might be the right thing for them, or at the very least give CrossFit an extremely massive thank you for helping my doctor bill to stay at an even $0. There tends to be a reputation of overall coldness and smugness given to the CrossFit community that I have yet to experience for myself, despite visiting many gyms around the country. On the contrary, the people I have met in these gyms have been the kindest, most courageous, loving people, many of whom will be lifetime friends. In my travels I've had the honor of being mentored and coached by amazing people from a vast variety of backgrounds. I have trained with Olympic lifting coaches, world class powerlifting coaches, gymnasts, CrossFit Games champions, and men and women who have served our country in the military. Everyone brings with them their own stories and backgrounds, and when working together to complete difficult tasks, it is a great and true honor to witness the ways in which each of their stories weave together to help others on their journeys.

Now for the harder things, which are also the most gratifying. The following are questions maybe you've wanted to ask but never knew who to reach out to, or where to find credible information on. I am not claiming that my experience is the authority by any means, but it is an honest, personal account for your consideration. Specifically, it is a very short summary of the logistics side that I wish I had when I started. I've outlined some discussion around common concerns, including a breakdown of many of the different terms, jargon, and movements. I've also added ways to modify many of these movements if needed. And, I can tell you if you're just starting it is absolutely encouraged to modify and do what you can, rather than trying to do what others are doing. All of the above are questions and concerns I had when I was starting out, but did not have anyone to talk to without feeling self-conscious about it. It did't feel very great to have to ask hundreds of questions about basic things, and as soon as I got home from a workout, I forgot 99% of the things I wanted to search on the internet. But what I found even when I did remember, was that there was not a single point of reference for any of these basic things. Here, I am hoping to fix that. At least a little.

CHAPTER 2

The Who And The What

A FEW THINGS TO EXPECT AND A FEW THINGS TO HELP YOU GET BETTER

At the heart of the CrossFit community we have the following:

"Constantly varied functional movements executed at high intensity across broad time and modal domains, with the stated goal of improving fitness, which it defines as work capacity across broad time and modal domains. Eat meat and vegetables, nuts and seeds, some fruit, little starch and no sugar. Keep intake to levels that will support exercise but not body fat."
GREG GLASSMAN, CrossFit Founder

YOU WON'T KNOW ANYTHING FOR A WHILE

Perhaps a long while. Enjoy being new. Rejoice because this is the one timeframe in your journey during which you are expected to suck, and your coaches will give you permission to continue to suck for a while. Whether it's sucking wind 99% of the time, sucking at every lift you try, or even sucking at remembering where the jump ropes are, remember that this is all absolutely okay. The lifts will feel awkward and the empty barbell will feel HEAVY. You'll have to ask around to find where certain pieces of equipment are located, you'll hear the same queues over and over while learning the movements, and it will feel like learning a new language. You are, in every respect, learning a new language. Remember that your body has to learn this language too.

Embrace it, and try to remember what it is like to be new, because all too soon you will be the one that new members will come to with their deer in the headlight questions. You'll be way ahead of the game if you are able to step into a mentoring role to help others out by remembering what it is like to be the new person on the floor.

THE GEAR PARADE

There's a boatload of CrossFit specific gear out there, with new versions coming out all the time. And for good reason. Our shoes are battered and slammed hour in and hour out, our hands get ripped and torn, or shins get scraped, our sweat gets in our eyes, and our jump ropes wear down to the bare metal in no time. Much of the mainstream gear available today is built to withstand the sheer volume demanded of it over time, so it's important to know what exactly you'll need before you dump a small fortune into things you don't.

A tried and true nugget of advice is to start with a good pair of shoes that feel comfortable for you, even if they are not specifically geared towards CrossFit. You'll want to make sure to slowly build up your leg strength, and this includes ensuring that your feet are housed in shoes that feel good and can sustain your lower half for running, jumping, squatting, and lunging. Try not to get too caught up in the endless internet searches for shoes, jump ropes, state of the art hoodies, and fancy leggings in the beginning, and definitely do not purchase more than a couple of articles of clothing at a time. Just go with what you have, such as an old t-shirt, tank top, and pair of board shorts or leggings as these will do just fine. You'll find that certain articles work better than others, so it's generally a good idea to try something out, see how it fits/works, and go from there.

Ask your coaches what their favorites have been, and why. Other members who have been around a while have likely gone through many types of gear themselves, so it's a good idea to ask the general population what their experience has been as well. Most importantly, find out what brands last for the long haul, and which one's shred to pieces after one set of rope climbs.

Once you've been practicing for a while, you can move into more specialized shoes and other gear if you like, and you can make educated choices based on the features you find necessary for you.

NOTES ON CLOTHING

In general, clothing should be loose enough to move about freely, whatever that means for you. Avoid shirts that are too loose and get in the way of the barbell or jump rope, and make sure your bottoms of choice will not fall down or rip. Jewelry of any kind should be left in a safe place away from the action.

Avoid lifting belts and hand grips until absolutely necessary, as you'll want to train your core and grip strength slowly without assistance. Your hands and forearms in particular will thank you if you can build up strength as much as possible without straps or gloves.

You may utilize chalk to help with slipping on the bar, ropes, kettlebells, or pull-up rig when your mitts get sweaty. Chalk is cheap, a good gym will allow it, (gasp!) and eventually you may not find a need for it once your hands become strong as vices.

Keep in mind that your goal in the beginning months will be to keep things simple, and set yourself up in a sustainable way to focus on learning the "basics" which in themselves are complicated enough.

HAND CARE

Speaking of hands, make sure to take meticulous care of your paws, since you'll need them for everything you do here.

You'll likely develop brag worthy calluses, but you'll want to keep these guys filed down low with a pumice stone and apply lotion nightly in order to avoid tearing. A torn set of calluses after a long set of kettlebell work has brought me to tears in the past (mainly tears of rage when experiencing the hot water of a simple shower afterwards, and how similar to salt in an open wound it was).

Best practice is to avoid torn calluses at all costs by taking some time to file them down and keep them soft. Healthy, strong mitts make for happy lifters in the gym. Bloody, aching palms however, result in much unnecessary anger and frustration. Try to avoid the latter.

SORENESS. A LOT OF IT

Yes, you can expect to be sore. You will soon be made keenly aware of muscles and connective tissue you didn't know existed, and sitting back into a chair or onto the toilet will be a historic journey altogether. My advice is to pound the fish oil capsules, get a good magnesium supplement, and take turmeric regularly. All of these things eat away at inflammation and will help you to bounce back faster. Another piece of advice on soreness: do not stay stagnant. The common recommendation for someone just starting out is to try and make it to the gym 2-3 days a week tops, with breaks in between workouts anywhere from 2-3 days. This helps ensure that a beginner does not get burnt out or injured, by giving the body time to bounce back. This does not however, mean one should go into full on rest mode. Instead, on your off days it will help immensely to go on a few short, easy walks throughout the day to keep things moving. If you cannot get out into the fresh air, make it a point to stand up every half hour or so and take a walk around the office. Do a set of 5 air squats every time you have to use the restroom, or a few toe to overhead reaches. Although it may be painful to move around, sitting still will make soreness worse. Don't forget to move.

LOCAL COMPETITIONS AND LIFTING MEETS

Eventually you'll see various competitions and lifting meets in your area. Try to attend these whenever possible, even if just to watch. As with anything you are learning, it can be very inspiring to watch people who have been doing it for a long time (and with many competitions, people who are just starting, like you!). It is also a great way to offer support and encouragement for people who have put a lot of hard work into an area that you too are working hard at.

Strength really does come in numbers, and supporting your local fellow athletes in a competition is a huge boost for both your own journey as well as theirs.

Eventually you might want to ease into it further by volunteering to judge or keep score. Even offering to help take the weights on and off the barbell during an Olympic meet is a great way to get to know people and coaches from around the nation (and it's a fantastic workout too). As you progress, think about signing up for a competition as a competitor. Many gyms will have partner competitions, which are a great way to ease into the pressure of an event along with someone else.

CHAPTER 3

The What Ifs:

ADDRESSING COMMON CONCERNS

It is understood that there are many concerns and reservations folks may have when considering whether or not CrossFit is for them. I've included the following as my take on some of the things I've heard throughout my journey just in case you may have wondered the same. I too threw around these questions, and would have liked to have been able to talk to someone before joining to get a take on them. Instead, I found out on my own, which may just be the key to addressing most concerns in the end. Ultimately, here are some thoughts on commonly asked questions. Feel free to dig further if you'd like!

WHY DOES IT COST SO MUCH?

Some individuals are concerned about the membership fees being expensive compared to other gyms. This is true, CrossFit memberships are expensive. Try to look at this from a standpoint of receiving custom, one-on-one coaching each and every time you attend a session. For all time. In contrast, many personal trainers at your typical big box $30 a month gym charge over $100 an hour just to show you the weight machines, give you a generic training plan, some meal recipes, and then you're on your own. Unless of course you want to pay another $100 for one additional hour next week.

Good coaches at a CrossFit gym will meticulously watch out for each individual no matter what level they are at, every single hour you are in their care. Due to the many details involved in each movement at the gym, you will not find your coach in a corner on their phone checking the weather or posting selfies, but instead it is expected that they remain engaged with each student throughout the workout and offer guidance accordingly. They will give specialized queues, tips, and adjustments as needed and in accordance with an athlete's physiology and mobility.

This is absolutely the very opposite of one size fits all cookie cutter coaching you might find at a regular gym. Many of these coaches are trained and certified in specialty areas in addition to their required CrossFit Training, such as the Olympic lifts, kettlebells, powerlifting and mobility.

Another way to break this down is cost per training session. If a membership is $150 per month, and you attend 6 days a week, that's just over $6 per session for world class coaching and a programmed set of workouts that do not require you to think about what to do next. Just show up, and follow what is on the white board for that day. Unlike knocking out a few reps on the squat machine before hitting up the stair master for cardio, you'll find that the constantly varied workouts prescribed by your coach and performed as a group will build and progress over time, even if they do seem random and disjointed. You will soon understand the importance of showing up more often than not, simply because you won't want to miss out on the chance to practice these drills as much as possible to continually improve upon them. Unlike the treadmill with a built in flatscreen that shows you a depressing news story on repeat, daily sessions with your CrossFit coach and fellow gym members will be well worth the money spent each month. Do not make the mistake of allowing the higher cost discourage you before giving it a try.

One option that many people take advantage of, is a gym's willingness to work with their students to ensure that everyone can participate. Depending on the gym, you may find ways to earn your membership in creative ways. Ask your coaches if they offer discounts for students, couples, or military. Some gyms will waive the fees entirely if one decides to become a CrossFit Trainer and coach at the gym throughout the week. Other gyms may give generous discounts to those who offer to jump on the weekly gym cleaning rotation (this also doubles as an excellent workout just from moving all of that heavy stuff around!). As you can see, there are many ways in which to offset the pricing if you are open to asking.

WHAT IF I GET HURT?

Yep, injuries have the potential to happen no matter what kind of physical activity is being performed. An unconditioned person can snap an achilles tendon while taking off after their dog down the street, or throw their back out when picking up a small child. The two questions that come to mind are: Are you content with risking an injury due to inactivity, or would you rather try easing into functional movement in a controlled, safe setting, to avoid such an injury in the first place? As with anything, the key here is to let the body learn its way into the work slowly. Bones, muscles, and connective tissue all have a lot of new things to learn, so it is ideal if these things can be done slowly and carefully.

On the flip side, if you suddenly have to jump out of the way of a car, you won't have the luxury of easing into any of that slowly. You're going to load your leg muscles, joints, tendons, and tissue, and hope that your springs don't snap upon take off or landing. At the gym however, you can use the combination of your level of comfortability with a movement, along with your coach's assessment of what you can handle, to safely guide the body to become strong in a vast variety of everyday movements.

Think of each session, each movement, and each repetition as practice rather than an all out race to the finish line. The race can and will come later, but right now in the beginning, your task is to slowly get the body accustomed to these new movements.

You'll have plenty of time to let the arrow fly once your body is ready.

THEY'RE NOT DOING THE SAME THINGS ON ANY GIVEN DAY; HOW DOES ANYONE GET BETTER?

Remember the entire purpose here is this:

"Constantly varied functional movements executed at high intensity across broad time and modal domains," with the stated goal of improving fitness, which it defines as "work capacity across broad time and modal domains."

The whole point is to get the body accustomed to being able to do a variety of different things, at a variety of intensities, with the goal of improving fitness overall. The really magical thing about performing so many different tasks in a given week, is the ability to see what specific things you are prone to enjoy the most. One can then take these findings and tweak them as the journey unfolds such as signing up for an obstacle race, joining an Olympic lifting team, Power lifting team, or running a distance race. Then, as you discover the things you may not enjoy as much, you'll soon know the feelings of accomplishment and power that come hand in hand with mastering something truly difficult. It's an addictive feeling, and there is no shortage of opportunities here. Embrace them

CHAPTER 4

The What Now:

A TOOLBOX FOR MIND AND BODY

There are a few things I learned through trial and error over the last several years of the journey, and it was hard not to include them when compiling this book. I say this because I know everyone who begins anything new (not just a path within CrossFit) will likely encounter some or all of these points as they go. Here are some thoughts to reflect on when starting anything for the first time, and may be useful to come back to later on.

DO YOU FIRST

You'll have a lot to take in during the first few months and sometimes longer, so don't get too caught up in what other people are doing right away. Eventually as you progress, you'll find certain people whom you may look to as role models or for support, but in the beginning, it will be tough to discern one person from the next based on a few moments of observation. Instead, pay attention to the important things, namely your coach, because you're not going to know if the others around you are doing the movements correctly anyway. Best not to copy them, and consult your coach instead.

Make a point to focus on counting your reps accurately, because you'll find that the ability to keep track in your head may be fleeting during a set of 100 jumps over a rope or 30 burpees. It's easy to get lazy with your counting and revert to finishing up when everyone else does. Do not short yourself here, and complete the work as prescribed by your coach, without shortcuts. It is also very important to note the queues given as you're learning a new lift, work on getting your body to actually follow them, and retain them for next time.

TRACK YOUR PROGRESS

Record your numbers, your times, your weights for various lifts, and major accomplishments like your first double unders or kipping pull-ups. Bring a notebook with you if you need, and I encourage you to jot down the weights and numbers as you are starting, so that you can track your progress as you go along. This is a highly powerful exercise in itself, to be able to look back at a former best lift, and beat it. You'll find it empowering to know that you lifted x amount in the deadlift last month, and record 20 pounds more than that the next time. For this reason, I've included additional space within the pages of this book, so that you may have one centralized place to note these items as you achieve them.

KNOW WHERE YOUR METAL IS

An extremely vital area in which to pay attention is where you're letting the equipment fall, and where your focus is when the bar or anything else is over your head.

In other words:

1) Don't let anything drop to the deck without stepping out of the way.

2) When doing any overhead movement, whether it be with the bar, kettlebell, or dumbell, pay attention to where these pieces of equipment are at all times. I

3) If the movement requires you to fix your gaze on something other than said piece of equipment, for the sake of all that is right in the world, please keep your focus on the location of that equipment.

4) More often than not, you're going to have a heavy piece of iron over your head. You want to know where it is at all times, period.

"THEY" ARE NOT WATCHING YOU

Remember, everyone else is working too hard and sweating too much to pay attention to what anyone else is doing (unless of course it's a high five and congratulations on completing a tough workout). Despite thinking they might be watching you like hawks, they're not. Not even a little bit.

And if they are watching you, they're either the coach and that's their job, or they are not the coach and they are not doing their job (which is working hard enough to not pay attention to anything else). Even with all of this said, you'll still experience the paranoia of Strongman Sven staring you down while you complete your fifth set of 30 burpees, but you'll soon realize that you don't even hear what music is playing when you're in the middle of a tough set of work like that. So, rest assured that the last thing you'll remember is what the person next to you was doing, and you can be certain they won't remember the details of what you did either (unless it is a celebratory high five for a job well done at the end of course).

WHAT YOU FOCUS ON GROWS -

There are many things to learn here, so to keep from being overwhelmed, try to find the movements and lifts you enjoy the most, and that you are naturally good at. Some people are fantastic at the dead lift out of the gate but are slower on the rowing machine, while others may be extremely fast runners but yet might have a harder time moving the big weights off the floor. People with shorter limbs and torsos might blow the pants off of the taller folks in their speed for burpees and ability to move heavy weights overhead, while the taller individuals may find it way more efficient to row a fast 800 meter or jump the first leg of a rope climb almost half way up from the start. Of course, there is no actual way to categorize what a given person will be good at or need to work harder to improve on, but these points are meant to get you thinking in terms of how you might use what you've got to your advantage once you get a feel for what works easily, and what might need extra attention.

In the beginning it is especially helpful to give yourself a mental boost by putting a LOT of positive thought towards the things you gravitate to, and then working on the rest with increased intensity as you get better. The nice thing about CrossFit workouts, is that you'll always be required to do the things that you dislike at one point or another, so there's no escaping those things anyway and you may as well be thankful for when something you are good at is scrawled across Captain Whiteboard!

OTHER PEOPLE AT THE GYM

When you start getting into the groove of things, you're probably going to pinpoint those who are extremely good at every. Thing. Once you're feeling like you have some footing, try to see these beasts as examples to strive towards, rather than letting it get you down for not keeping up. They were new once too, they get it! Furthermore, you'll start noticing that newer people will come along who are similar to where you were when you started. Try to help give them a positive and encouraging experience by greeting them by name when they come in, cheering them on, helping them out if it looks like they might need a high five, or even finishing up the end of a workout with them if you've completed it sooner and they are the last ones.

These little things can have a huge impact on a new member's experience and for the gym as a whole. I believe that if each person makes an effort to smile and be an overall positive influence, the more people we will have to champion the integrity of our CrossFit community.

YOU GOT THIS

Pick a number, put it in your head, and stick with it. Whether it's setting the clock for 5AM and forcing yourself to open your eyes to get out of bed rather than hitting snooze, setting a number of 5 days per week to hit up the gym, setting a number of 20 wall balls before setting the medicine ball down, or pushing through an 800 meter row before slowing down.

Put a number in your head, and stick to it. Let that number resonate in your mind when the muscles are aching and the lungs are hurting. You'll thank yourself next time the same exercise comes across your plate, because you'll know that you've already done it and can do it again.

Remember, consistency over the long term will result in continual improvement.

FOR CRYING OUT LOUD HAVE FUN

This isn't a contest to the death. No one is going to knock you down and steal your shoes if you trip up on your jump rope for the tenth time today. The best part about working together with people who are in the middle of the same struggles as you is that you can glance over at your neighbor, cheer them on, and smile when it's done knowing you did more work in one hour than 99% of the population does in a week.

CHAPTER 5

The How To:

GLOSSARY OF TERMS

One thing I had a tough time with, was remembering all of the terms, lingo, and names of things in general once I left the gym. Hard work sometimes clouds the brain for a little while after all. The worst part was that I found it difficult to remember the names of the people I met, and that's kind of important. So, here is a list of terms so that you can work on learning the names of your fellow athletes first and foremost, and save the lingo for home research.

Here, for your enjoyment and education is list for reference at a glance.

AMRAP: A workout type that stands for "as many rounds as possible" in a given amount of time. For example, count the number of pushups you can do in 5 minutes. One might see "AMRAP 10 (5 push-ups, 5 pull-ups). In this case one would keep track of how many sets of 5 push-ups and 5 pull-ups completed during 10 minutes.

Assault bike: A variation on the stationary bike, this little devil of a chariot on wheels packs a huge metabolic hit while recruiting the arms and legs to push, pull, and pedal one's way to nowhere. Typical units of measurement are distance and calories burned. Tip for the assault bike: If the legs start burning, compensate by pushing heavier with your arms. If the arms start to give out, help them out by pedaling harder with the legs for a little while. The beauty about this beast is the ability to adjust where your power is coming from. Just remember, "Arms and legs, arms and legs, arms and legs"

Barbell: The glistening, sometimes rusty metal rod of glory on which bumper plates are placed for lifting. This staple will become your best friend, mortal enemy, and invaluable mentor in the days and years to come. Treat it with respect, but know that if you absolutely must curse at it, that is completely acceptable to do so. Just remember to say you're sorry afterward. Weight of the barbell for men is 20 kilograms (44 pounds) and 15 kilograms (33 pounds) for women.

Below parallel: This is a position in the squat movement where the hip crease ends up below the knees. Not everyone will have the mobility to squat this low to the deck. Your coach will be able to work with you to find what best suits your anatomy in the squat movements.

Box: A term used to refer to a CrossFit gym. Since many gyms are set up within industrial areas and are fairly bare boned and to the point, the term 'Box 'is quite fitting.

Box Jump: A jump from the ground onto a regular old (yet very stable) wooden box, or any other elevated surface. Pay attention to what you are doing on this one, as it is quite common to catch a toe or otherwise end up with missing skin from the shins as a result of a fall. This movement is typically performed onto a 20-inch or 24-inch box, however can be performed at any height. Anyone who may be unfamiliar with a higher jump can easily start with just a few inches off the ground by using a bumper plate, and working their way up. Literally. Some gyms may have a softer version of the wooden box for those learning as well. These are usually made of a foam interior, and are fantastic on the joints for a softer landing, and of course, easing into the movement without as much risk of a shin skin grabber.

Bumper plates: Round, virtually indestructible donuts of mighty capacity, these are weights that are used for placing on a barbell. They are made of materials that are a bit softer (instead of plain metal) so that when dropping they are not as hard on the surface flooring. You'll notice many different use cases for these off the bar as well. Plates can be carried overhead for distance, grasped between the fingers to train grip strength, placed overhead for adding weight to a sit- up, or even chained around the waist for added resistance in a pull-up.

Burpee: Your go-to, all body, no equipment required tool in the box. This is a series of movements starting with the standing position. Squat down, place the hands on the floor on either side of the feet, move the legs back into a push up position, move legs back up into a squatting position, stand, and finally jump up to an overhead clapping of the hands. Legs can either walk back into and out of the pushup position, or can jump back. Depending on a person's tolerance for impact, this one can easily be scaled by using the walk back method, and will still be a very effective way to increase the heart rate and engage all muscles of the body. When traveling, do a set of 200 in the mornings from your hotel room, or hit the deck in the airport and knock out as many as you can while waiting for your next connection. When you're unable to make it to the gym, the burpee will not disappoint in terms of getting a full body workout in a short amount of time. You've got your squats and pushups covered, along with the huge metabolic hit that comes along with quickly getting down to the ground and back up again repeatedly.

Butterfly: Watching someone execute this movement well is quite awe inspiring. This is a variation of the pull-up, and gets its name from how similar it is to the butterfly swimming technique, only while hanging from a pull-up bar. It is mainly used when the goal is to get through a long set of pull-ups quickly. Once mastered, it is an extremely efficient way to utilize the force of the hips to move the body upward for many repetitions. Due to the high workload placed on the hands, it is recommended to work up to this slowly rather than risk tearing.

Butterfly sit-up: A nice variation on the classic crunch. This movement starts in the seated position with the feet together and knees splayed outward towards the floor. Lay back to the floor behind you, move arms overhead to touch the floor overhead, and then sit back up, leaning back over the feet. Add a bumper plate or kettlebell for added resistance.

Captain Whiteboard: The board on which the WOD (workout of the day) is written for all to follow during the course of the next hour or so. Rather than barking orders, this guy silently instructs via dry erase marker fumes. It is just as effective, I might add.

Chipper: A workout type that requires for all repetitions of a movement to be done before moving to the next movement. An example might be: 50 air squats, 40 sit ups, 30 walking lunges, 20 push-ups, 10 pull-ups. Working/chipping away at the movements until completion is the name of the game. The good news is, once you finish with one movement you won't have to do it again (usually)!

Clean: A barbell lift that starts with the bar on the ground, and ends resting on the shoulders at the front of the neck. The bar movement is straight up the belly, keeping the hips low at first. There are many small details to this movement that can take a very long time to master, so do not get discouraged with this one!

Clean and jerk: One of two Olympic lifts, the other being the Snatch. This is a barbell movement with many small nuances, but in short it is taking the bar from the ground to the shoulders, and then powerfully moving it upwards above the head to lockout.

Deadlift: One of several power lifts involving the barbell. With many finer points to be discovered by each individual person, this one at the root level is raising the barbell from the ground up to the hips and setting it back down. There are entire books written about this movement alone, so do not let the simplicity illustrated here full you. Envision the arms as ropes and the hands as vices gripping the bar ferociously as you stand up with it. This is not a 'pull ' from the ground. It is a standing up forcefully while not letting the bar go.

Double Under: Jumping rope with a bit more wrist action. This movement requires for the jump rope to make two passes under the feet with each jump upward.

EMOM: A workout type that stands for "every minute on the minute." This simply means one would complete a designated amount of reps each minute. Using our trusty push-ups and pull ups combination, an example might be "EMOM 10 (5 pus-hups, 5 pull-ups). When the clock starts, one would complete 5 push-ups and 5 pull-ups, and rest for the remainder of the minute until the next minute starts. Wash, rinse, repeat for 10 minutes.

GHD machine: (glute ham developer) In many gyms this underused piece of equipment sits off on the sidelines. In fact, it is a wonderful way to strengthen the hamstrings, glutes, abs, and back, and aids in preventing hamstring strains and back injuries. Some of the common exercises done on this machine are: the hip and back extension, glute ham raise, and sit up. Hug a bumper plate close to your chest to add more resistance to your efforts on this one, and watch your core strength soar.

Handstand push-up: This is exactly how it sounds. A dizzying upside-down shoulder roaster, it is performed against a wall for balance. One starts in a handstand position and then lowers the head to the floor, and then pushes back up.

Hang: A barbell position where one stands with the barbell 'hanging 'by the hands. A use case for the hang would be a variation of the Clean. Instead of starting with the barbell on the ground, one starts at the hang position, takes a slight dip downwards, and moves the barbell up to the shoulders at the front of the neck to finish.

Hero WODs: (workout of the day) These workouts are tributes to a fallen first responders or members of the military. You might see a workout around Memorial Day for example, called "Murph." This one takes about an hour or less for people to complete and is comprised of a 1-mile run, 100 pull-ups, 200 push-ups, 300 air squats, and a 1 mile run to top it off. All while wearing a 20-pound weighted vest as if the work wasn't enough. Don't let it intimate you though. This is a phenomenal chance to test your progress annually by recording your time and trying to beat it next year.

Hopper: A workout type that is put together by sheer luck of the draw, such as using a deck of cards. An example might be: clubs = push-ups, diamonds = pull-ups, spades = air squats, hearts = burpees. If a 5 of hearts is drawn, everyone does 5 burpees. One might be surprised and perhaps horrified at the sheer amount of work involved in a 52-card deck of playing cards. No need to fear though, it'll all be over in an hour.

Kettlebell: A round piece of steel with a handle. Lovingly referred to as "cannon balls with handles" these minimalist pieces of equipment are a staple in many gyms, with an unlimited potential for variety. Typical movements with the kettlebell are: swings, snatches, cleans, squats, presses, and Turkish get-ups. There are entire certifications that athletes can acquire for kettlebells alone, so if you find yourself falling in love with these cold spheres of iron, you might want to research their full potential and find out what they are capable of with the right knowhow.

Kettlebell swing (American style): Kettlebell ends up overhead. Using one kettlebell with both hands, picture the movement required to hike a football back between the legs, followed by an explosive hip thrust to propel the bell forward and overhead, rather than stopping at eye level as with the traditional Russian style swing.

Kettlebell swing (Russian style): Kettlebell ends up at eye level. Using one kettlebell with both hands, picture the movement required to hike a football back between the legs, followed by an explosive hip thrust to propel the bell forward to eye level, rather than overhead as with the American style swing. For this reason, one can also add variety to the Russian swing by performing the above with one hand, switch between hands, or use double kettlebells. All of these movements have an astounding effect on the full body, firing up the hamstrings, glutes, abdominals, and shoulders. Typical prescribed weights for men are 53 pounds, and 35 pounds for women. This is base level, and most gyms will have a full range of kettlebells from 18 pounds going up to the 108-pound beast. Bells were originally measured in poods (one mood = 36 pounds) but you'll see them measured in pounds and kilograms these days.

Kipping pull-up: A variation on the pull-up, deriving from a combination of a 'kick 'and a 'pull-up. 'A fairly technical move to master, this form of a pull-up allows for many repetitions to be completed in a short amount of time. This movement utilizes momentum from the hips to move the body up to the pull-up bar while relying on the shoulders to hinge open and closed to complete the series. Because it relies more on the full body movement to be faster and more efficient, it is sometimes frowned upon by those who are hard core strict pull-up practitioners.

Masters: This refers to the "seniors" age division for CrossFit competitions. As of the writing of this book, there are six Masters divisions each for women and men: 35–39, 40–44, 45–49, 50–54, 55–59, and 60+. Divisions for teenagers were introduced in 2015 and the age ranges are 14–15 and 16–17, for both male and females.

Metcon: A workout term that is short for "metabolic conditioning." These types of workouts switch between cardio and strength. An example might be 20 deadlifts followed by a 200-meter run, repeated several times.

Muscle-up: A literal step up from the classic pull-up, this movement requires more of a gymnastic approach and is typically performed on a set of rings (this can also be done on a pull-up bar, referred to as a bar muscle-up). To complete this movement, one grips a set of rings overhead and pulls the body up forcefully, ending with the arms extended and rings at hip level. A complex movement that for most, requires many hours of practice. Do not fear though, there are many ways to scale this one.

Olympic lifts: Two lifts performed in the Olympics and other Olympic lifting meets, the Snatch and the Clean and Jerk.

Overhead Squat: With the barbell overhead and arms locked out in a wide grip, this is a lowering of the body by sitting the hips back as if to sit down into a chair, and lowering down towards the ground before rising back up.

Parallettes: Small bars that sit off the ground around 8 inches which are used for movements such as L-sits (legs outstretched in front of the body while the arms hold the body up a few inches off the ground) or for placing against the wall to allow for handstand push-ups to be more difficult (if there is such a thing!).

Pistol: A variation on the squat movement, done on one leg. From the side, the body looks like a pistol when in the bottom position because the leg not in use is outstretched to the front, while the working leg is bending close to the body. These movements can be done with bodyweight only, or weighted with a dumbbell, plate, or kettlebell to increase difficulty. This one is easily modified by placing a box close to the body to sit back onto, rather than having to lower all the way to the ground and back up.

Power Clean: A barbell lift that involves raising the bar from the floor to the shoulders in front of the neck, while landing in a partial squat instead of a full squat.

PR: Personal record. It can be extremely gratifying to start writing down your workouts on a calendar or in a notebook when you begin your journey. You can then look back at where you started, and compare how far you've come. For this reason, I've left bonus room within the pages of this book in case you would like to record some of these numbers here.

Prowler: Also referred to as a sled. These metal contraptions with handles are loaded with weight plates and pushed across the ground for a set distance, turned around, and pushed back. The wind is taken out of the sails quickly with a heavy sled push, as it requires much output from the larger muscle groups of the quads.

Rig: A term used to refer to the overall steel structures that support barbells for lifting and pull-up bars.

Rope climb: Climbing up a rope and back down. These can be done using arms only, or practiced with the legs clamped around the rope to help propel one upward. There are many scaling options for these so do not worry or let this one intimidate you; you'll get there!

Rower: Most all CrossFit gyms have rowing machines. A fantastic way to recruit all muscle groups and obtain a no-impact high metabolic hit. Typical units of measurement are distance, wattage/output, and calories. If running is too hard on your joints, or if an injury is nagging at you, the rower can be used in place of running until the body is ready for more impact

Rx'd: Short for "as prescribed" as in, doing the workout at the recommended weights without scaling back or modifying.

Sandbags: Ranging from 10-70 pounds typically, sandbags are a great addition to running. Some workouts may incorporate the sandbag for squats, shoulder toss overs, and various barbell movement replacements to train grip and handling of oddly shaped objects.

Scaled: The ability (and in most cases, the recommendation) to modify any workout to fit the needs of each individual. This could mean jumping pull-ups instead of strict, knees on the floor push-ups, lowering the weight for lifts, stepping up onto a box instead of box jumps or rowing instead of running. Most every athlete with the exception of the elites will scale in one way or another, so you will be in good company when your coach instructs you to scale as well.

Ski erg: This is a piece of equipment that is best described as a vertical rowing machine. The mechanics are similar, however instead of sitting down and going through a rowing motion, one stands up and pulls the handles from overhead to the floor, as if downhill skiing. Measurements are typically distance, watts, or calories.

Snatch: One of two Olympic lifts, the other being the Clean and Jerk. The barbell is pulled from the ground with a very wide grip, and quickly turned overhead in one movement while landing in a partial or full squat. The movement ends when the body and arms are at a full lockout overhead. This is a highly technical, if not the most technical lift you'll do, so take the time to learn and practice it well.

Strict pull-up: Pulling the body upward to the bar starting at a complete hang, with no kipping movement to assist. Once the neck is level with the bar, the body is then lowered back down to a dead hang. Pull-ups can be scaled in many different ways, so do not be discouraged if this is a no go at first. One may begin by placing a box or series of bumper plates beneath the bar, and jumping the body up to neck level with the bar. When a long set of these becomes doable, one might transition to a banded pull-up. Many gyms have bands of various thicknesses available for use in a variety of different ways, and this is a great way to help develop strength in a pull-up. The idea is to take weight off the body by placing the foot or knee in the loop of a band that has been wrapped onto the top of the pull-up bar. When performing the movement, the resistance of the band works like a person giving you a literal hand up to the bar. As your strength builds, you can decrease the size and resistance of the band, until you no longer need one at all to perform the movement.

Squat clean: A barbell lift that starts with the bar on the ground, and ends resting on the shoulders at the front of the neck with legs in a full squat position. The lift ends with standing up to full body lockout.

Tabata: A fast workout type consisting of 20 seconds of all out work (to the point of not being able to talk to your neighbor) followed by a 10 second "rest" which never seems to last long enough before going into the next 20 seconds of work. This sequence is repeated 8 times totaling 4 minutes of work. The magic of this beauty comes with the intensity with which the athlete performs during the 20 seconds of work. Those 20 seconds are meant to be utilized as an all out, full capacity block of work during which one should not be able to muster up the ability to form words.

Thruster: Once referred to as the devil's asshole, this barbell movement begins in a full squat with the barbell resting at the shoulders in front of the neck, with elbows pointed to the sky as much as possible. One then rises to standing while pressing the bar overhead in one solid movement. Wash, rinse, repeat for a set of 10 and you'll soon understand the nickname.

Tires: Good old farm equipment tires have been a staple at many gyms, mainly used for rolling, flipping, or slamming with sledgehammers. A good, wholesome way to take out any aggression or stress from a hard day at the office, these things won't complain or mope or backtalk, no matter what you do to them.

Toes to Bar: Starting at a hang from the pull-up bar, the toes are raised to tough the bar between the hands. Scaling options for this movement include: raising just the knees as high up as possible, or lying on the ground perpendicular to the rig with hands holding onto the rig overhead.and raising the legs up to touch the rig.

Turkish get-up: An all body movement typically performed with a kettlebell. Simply put, with the kettlebell locked out overhead, the practitioner will get down onto the ground, onto their back and back up again, or vice versa by starting on the floor first and going through the same sequence. The finer details take some getting used to, but if we were to break it down into a few steps they would be: Start on your back, with a kettlebell in your right arm held locked out above your head. Do not take your eyes off the bell. Bend the same knee as the arm holding the bell. Thrust your core upward, so that you are propped up on the opposite forearm (in this case, the left forearm). Shoot the hips up, so that the body is in a plank, and then get yourself onto your left hand as your left arm is supporting the weight. The left (non-bent) leg then swings behind you like a windshield wiper, positioning itself so that the body may rise up into a lunge with the right leg in front and left leg behind. Come to full standing with both legs straight. Step back with the left leg and do the entire process in reverse. This is a good one to observe as a seasoned practitioner performs the movement, so that you can get a good visual before practicing on your own. A great way to practice is to use a shoe or something light in place of the kettlebell to get a feel for the sequence before placing a ball of iron overhead.

Wall ball: A medicine ball ranging in weight from 6 to 30 pounds (usual weights for women are 14 pounds, 20 pounds for men) which is thrown overhead against a wall to hit a target 9-10 feet high). The ball is then caught in a full squat before being launched upward again, repeatedly for the duration of the workout or prescribed number of repetitions.

WOD: Workout of the day. As soon as you arrive at the gym, your eyes will gravitate over to the ever present oracle of a whiteboard, on which the WOD will be inscribed. Some gyms may have the WOD projected for all to see on a fancy flat screen, however most places will still use ye olde Captain Whiteboard for simplicity sake.

CHAPTER 6

The Where From:

QUOTES AND SAYINGS

Often times it takes just a line or a saying in order that one might get that final kick in the pants they need to make a change, and more importantly, keep it. Here, I've included some nuggets of high voltage words to end this book on a powerful note and hopefully add more color to some of the more subtle hints that are scattered within the previous pages, in case you missed them.

My favorite of all time, is this:

MOTIVATION IS EXTERNAL.
MOTIVATION DOES NOT LAST
DISCIPLINE COMES FROM
WITHIN.

DISCIPLINE IS A REQUIREMENT
FOR WHEN MOTIVATION NO
LONGER EXISTS.

IF IT'S IMPORTANT, DO IT EVERY
DAY.

I AM THE MASTER OF MY
THOUGHTS, AND THEREFORE I
BECOME WHAT I THINK ABOUT.
THIS TRUE FOR THE GOOD OR THE
BAD. YOU CHOOSE WHICH YOU
WANT TO BECOME.

CREATE THE VERSION OF YOUR
BEST SELF IN YOUR MIND FIRST,
AND THEN DO THE WORK TO GET
THERE. SHOW UP AS THE PERSON
YOU CREATE IN YOUR MIND.

IT HURTS NOW BUT ONE DAY IT
WILL BE YOUR WARM UP

EASY DOESN'T MAKE YOU PROUD.

WHEN YOU CHANGE THE WAY
YOU LOOK AT THINGS, THE
THINGS YOU LOOK AT CHANGE.

PUT A NUMBER IN YOUR HEAD,
AND GET THERE.

YOU BECOME WHAT YOU THINK
ABOUT. THINK ONLY OF YOUR
STRENGTHS, NOT YOUR
WEAKNESSES.

SHOW UP. ONCE YOU'RE HERE,
YOUR MIND AND BODY WILL DO
THE REST.

CONCLUSION

Thank you so very much for your time in reading this book.!

I hope the content here was able to help answer some of your questions about CrossFit, and provide a decent knowledge base to assist in your path going forward, whatever it may be..

Finally, if you enjoyed this book, I would like to ask you for a favor. Would you be kind enough to leave a review for this book on Amazon? I would greatly appreciate your feedback for future iterations of this book, and publications to come.

Thank you once again for taking the time to visit this content. I send to you powerful thoughts as you continue your journey to let your arrow fly.

Heidi Leatherby

Notes

TOPIC: